PAUL WHITEMAN

666
AND ALL THAT

Copyright © 2021 Paul Whiteman

The moral right of the author has been asserted.

Apart from any fair dealing for the purposes of research or private study, or criticism or review, as permitted under the Copyright, Designs and Patents Act 1988, this publication may only be reproduced, stored or transmitted, in any form or by any means, with the prior permission in writing of the publishers, or in the case of reprographic reproduction in accordance with the terms of licences issued by the Copyright Licensing Agency. Enquiries concerning reproduction outside those terms should be sent to the publishers.

Matador
9 Priory Business Park,
Wistow Road, Kibworth Beauchamp,
Leicestershire. LE8 0RX
Tel: 0116 279 2299
Email: books@troubador.co.uk
Web: www.troubador.co.uk/matador
Twitter: @matadorbooks

ISBN 978 1800461 802

British Library Cataloguing in Publication Data.
A catalogue record for this book is available from the British Library.

Printed and bound in Great Britain by 4edge Limited
Typeset in 10.5pt Adobe Jenson Pro by Troubador Publishing Ltd, Leicester, UK

Matador is an imprint of Troubador Publishing Ltd

Acknowledgements

I am indebted to my wife, Janet Whiteman, for her help and encouragement. I thank her for many useful suggestions, for checking manuscripts – and for generally keeping me going.

The London Library was extremely helpful during the 2020 coronavirus pandemic by providing postal loans of relevant reference books, which were virtually unobtainable elsewhere. I thank the Library colleagues for their consideration and kindness in the face of the difficulties.

Similarly, I am also most grateful to the people at Troubador Publishing Ltd. for their professionalism and efficiency, and patience, in helping me publish via the Matador imprint.

Contents

Preface		ix
1.	The Number of the Beast	1
2.	What's in a Number?	4
3.	Beliefs about Numbers	16
4.	The Numbers of Time	29
5.	The Revelation of St. John	35
6.	Sixes and Sevens	54
7.	Mindset	63
8.	Apocalypse When?	69
Bibliography		75
Index		79

Preface

666 is an ancient number, or code, that has diverse religious and occult meanings. Some years ago, I discovered that a particular version of this number had an interesting property, one which could be interpreted as a message. The scary events associated with this 'revelation' prompted me to investigate further the strange world of mystical numbers and apocalyptic messages.

This small book aims to document my relatively trivial finding and to put it into context. The associated mathematical, religious, esoteric and scientific backgrounds deserve books in their own right to do them justice. Some pertinent reference sources are listed in the bibliography section. I apologise in advance to those who may feel that important issues have been omitted or misrepresented. My tentative interpretations and conclusions should not be taken out of context.

Chapter 1
The Number of the Beast

This particular journey into the weird world of mystical numbers and apocalyptic messages began on a May night in 1992. In the early hours, I woke abruptly with a severe attack of asthma. My wife rushed me in the car to the local accident and emergency department. Thanks to modern medicine, and skilled doctors and nurses, I was pulled back from the brink. It was an unpleasant but not unfamiliar experience. By dawn I had been transferred to one of those mixed-sex general medical wards that were fashionable at the time in British NHS hospitals. Out of danger, and breathing easier, I began to dwell on the night's events. The coincidences were intriguing – in fact, a bit frightening.

On the evening before it all happened I was doodling with pen and paper. For some completely inexplicable reason I decided to analyse the number 666, the biblical number of the Antichrist. Within a few minutes I discovered that 666 had a unique self-contained mathematical property, one that led to another set of numbers – numbers of particular interest. But what was the significance, if any, of the finding? It was nearly midnight, so I decided to go to bed and to leave the conundrum for another day. I had just fallen asleep when a loud clap of thunder startled me back to consciousness. A violent storm was raging immediately overhead. The thunder shook the house with such force that I was compelled to check for damage. The storm was short-lived and I returned to bed around 2am. I awoke an hour later, blue and gasping for breath.

These events were probably not all coincidental. As a doctor, I knew that severe atmospheric disturbances, such as occur with thunder storms, can sometimes precipitate asthma. But could they possibly be connected with something else, such as my dabbling in the occult? My scientific training, and secularist tendency, persuaded me to analyse the situation rationally before jumping to silly conclusions.

I tried to relax in the hubbub of the ward and to think of other things. I was grateful to be alive. Then the bedside locker attracted my attention. Automatically, my hand reached out to the drawer. Inside it was one of those Gideon Bibles. I fumbled quickly through the pages at the end of the book. There it was, in Revelation 13[18]:

> '…. *If anyone has insight, let him calculate the number of the beast, for it is man's number. The number is 666.*'

I began reading other passages in the Book of Revelation. The more I read, the more disturbed I became. My calculation appeared to have more significance than I had originally thought. I quickly returned the book to the drawer. By now I was feeling agitated and nauseated, and then started to vomit. I soon realised that my new symptoms were probably due to aminophylline, which was still dripping into my arm via an intravenous cannula. The drug can be life-saving but it sometimes produces unpleasant side effects. I persuaded the house physician to stop the aminophylline infusion. The physical symptoms resolved in a few hours. But I was still apprehensive – in truth, a bit scared. Some weeks passed by before I could again bring myself to look at Revelation – also known as The Apocalypse.

Such experiences can lead superstitious and suggestible people down dark and dangerous paths of thought, which may be quite irrational. Survival often requires us to heed our most basic instincts. The facts upon which logical judgements can be made may not be available or may be unreliable. Inadequate or suspect evidence together with the persuasive pressures of one's own and others' beliefs often lead us to questionable conclusions. Often we are unsure about the truth of a situation and may have to rely upon such vagaries as probability, possibility, analogy, intuition or just plain faith. This applies not just to the fantastical aspects of religion and the occult but sometimes also to the heady frontiers of modern science. Whatever the truth about them, there is something compelling about mystical numbers and symbols. And they have greatly influenced the human mind.

What was my 666 calculation and what is its significance? More on that later. There are real dangers in dabbling in the occult. Each new thing we learn enhances our total store of knowledge. This may change our perception of the world and our reaction to it, sometimes slightly and sometimes profoundly. People are affected in different ways.

Chapter 2
What's in a Number?

In modern industrialised societies numbers operate mainly as servile concepts of quantity or of rank order. We use them to count and calculate, to rank and prioritise, to code and identify (e.g. bank accounts, pin numbers), and to measure things such as the dimensions of space and time. We regulate our lives by the numbers on the clock. Nowadays, many would regard the number as little more than an abstract construct of the human mind – part of the evolutionary process, an invention born of necessity. Like language, it improves the accuracy and efficiency of communication and transaction. But some ancient cultures and religions revered numbers as sacred entities in their own right. They attributed to them mystical, magical and even divine powers. Threads of these beliefs still persist today in the esoteric arts, such as numerology.

The Origin and Nature of Numbers

Our limited knowledge of ancient number systems comes largely from isolated archaeological discoveries and investigations made from the late 18th century onwards. At various times throughout history important information about the achievements of ancient civilisations has been ignored, lost, rewritten or even actively suppressed or destroyed. To this must be added the distorting effect of over-imaginative and sometimes bizarre interpretations of the few ancient written records that are still available for study (e.g. influence of beings from outer space). The popularity and book-selling potential of such ideas does not add weight to their validity. Despite all this, good scholarship has provided some seemingly sensible conclusions about the history of number.

For thousands of years before the advent of writing, humans communicated through some form of spoken language. This would have allowed them to pass on a gradually increasing body of knowledge and belief to future generations. During this prehistoric period humans also developed methods for counting and measuring – as evidenced from cairns and megalithic monuments. With the advent of writing some six thousand years ago the Sumerians began to record numbers as symbols on clay. About four to five thousand years ago relatively sophisticated arithmetic manipulations were being recorded by the Egyptians and Indians, and by the Babylonians, who absorbed Sumer and its culture around 2000 BC.

Evidence from early civilisations indicates that the development of numbers and arithmetic was a gradual process. The first recorded numerals resembled the less permanent methods of counting, such as fingers, piles of stones and marks in the sand, which had been used for millennia. Written records became an extension of the memory. They allowed the scribes responsible for them to think about more efficient ways of grouping and using numbers, as did the abacus and counting boards later on. The change from nomadic to more stable agrarian modes of life and the development of urban societies and state structures, with their increasing trade and wealth, fostered a need for more accurate and efficient methods of counting, calculation and record keeping. The design and erection of larger and more complex buildings, the use of astronomy and calendars for the prediction of seasonal events and increasingly adventurous navigation all spurred on the development of more sophisticated number systems and mathematical methods.

Features that make the current decimal number system suitable for complex calculations are:

- The use of different symbols for all numbers (1 to 9) less than the base value (ten).
- The concept of, and a symbol (0) for, zero.
- The use of place values to define larger numbers in an easily understood format. Take the decimal number 222. This means two hundred (2x10x10) plus twenty (2x10) plus 2.

Some of the earlier number systems were not easily amenable to procedures such as multiplication and division because they were deficient in some of these basic features. The Roman system of numerals, widespread in Europe until relatively recently, is an example of this problem. Try multiplying MCCCLXXIV by CCXCVIII! But, these handicaps did not deter some early civilisations from devising devices and procedures, including the use of ready-reckoner tables, for the calculation of products, quotients, squares, square roots, areas and volumes.

From about the 7th century AD, Arab scholars avidly studied and developed ideas from other cultures (Babylonian, Egyptian, Indian, Greek and Chinese). They made important advances that laid the foundations of Western mathematics and science. The mathematician Al-Khwarizmi (c. 680-750 AD) documented the Hindu-Arabic number system that we still use today. He also made major contributions to arithmetic and algebra. His name gave rise to the word 'algorithm'. Fibonacci (Leonardo da Pisa, c. 1170-1250 AD) is generally credited with the introduction of Hindu-Arabian mathematics into Europe through his *Liber Abaci* (Book of the Abacus, 1202 AD).

The ancient Greeks and Jews had a profound effect on Western thought – and on Christian thought in particular. Paradoxically, however, the awkwardness of their numbering systems together with their religious beliefs helped to retard the progress of mathematics in Europe for a thousand years. They used letter-numbers – the letters of their alphabets doubled up as symbols for a wide range of numbers (table 2.1). Therefore words and names could also be reduced to numbers. Both the Greeks and the Jews regarded numbers in two different ways. On the one hand, numerals could be used for everyday activities such as counting, trading and building. On the other hand, the numbers themselves and their arithmetic and geometric relationships, as concepts divorced from the material world, were held to be sacred and of great religious significance.

Table 2.1

Abbreviated list of Ancient Greek
and Hebrew letter-numbers

Hindu-Arabic Number	Alphabetic Equivalents (*): Greek	Hebrew
1	alpha	alef
2	beta	bet
3	gamma	gimel
4	delta	dalet
5	epsilon	he
6	zeta	vav
10	iota	yod
20	kappa	kaf
30	lambda	lamed
40	mu	mem
50	nu	nun
60	xi	samek
100	rho	qof
200	sigma	resh
300	tau	shin
400	upsilon	tav
500	phi	
600	chi	

(* Note: these are the names for the specific letter-number symbols – e.g. α = alpha; א = alef)

The Greek philosopher and mathematician Pythagoras (c. 580-500 BC) and his secret religious sect of followers, the

Pythagoreans, spent years pondering over, among other things, the mystical nature of numbers. Their influence lasted two thousand years and is still felt today. The elite of some orthodox religious organisations were deeply suspicious of new mathematical and scientific ideas and discoveries, especially those originating outside of their own circles.

When Europeans explored the Americas they found evidence of several ancient civilisations. The Mayan empire had been the most advanced but it went rapidly into decline in the 8th century – the reason for this is still debated. Their remarkable culture and amazing deserted city at Palenque in South Mexico, with its monumental pyramids and temples, were not studied properly until the 19th and 20th centuries. At its peak the Mayan civilisation had achieved a level of sophistication in mathematics and astronomy comparable to any contemporaneous civilisation. The Maya used a complex number system which underpinned their extraordinary measurements of time (table 4.1 in chapter 4).

The ancient civilisations of the Americas are generally assumed to have developed thousands of years in isolation from other continents. Arcane tradition points to Atlantis, a continent and great civilisation supposedly lost to the depths of the Atlantic Ocean some twelve thousand years ago, as a major influence on the development of later cultures, such as the Indian, Egyptian and Mayan civilisations. The possibility that peoples migrated from the Old World to the New World thousands of years ago cannot be completely discounted.

Rational and Irrational Numbers

In this book, thankfully, we shall concern ourselves only with *real numbers* and not the *imaginary numbers* (such as the square root of minus one) used in more abstract forms of mathematics. Real numbers are divided into *rational* and *irrational* numbers – the distinction is relevant. Put simply, a rational number is a whole number or a fraction made up of whole numbers (e.g. 6, 324, 3/8, 22/7) – it is finite. The world of the Pythagoreans revolved around rational numbers which they examined and compared in many different ways. This included an analysis of the submultiple factors of numbers. For instance, possible factors of 28, excluding 1, are 2, 4, 7 and 14 because they all divide exactly into 28. Factors of particular interest were the *prime numbers*, those that cannot be further divided exactly by any other whole number, apart from one and themselves – examples are 2, 3, 5, 7, 11, 13, 17 etc.

Six and 28 are examples of what the Geeks called *perfect numbers* because the sum of all their possible submultiple factors (including one) add up to the original number:

$$6 = 1 + 2 + 3$$
$$28 = 1 + 2 + 4 + 7 + 14$$

An *irrational number* is a real number that cannot be written in a form using whole number fractions. An example is the square root of 2 (1.414213…. ad infinitum). The number apparently goes on forever – the more decimal places added the nearer it gets to, but never reaches, the square root of two. This must not be confused with fractions that cannot be defined precisely in the decimal system, such as one third (1/3 = 0.33333….

recurring). Irrational numbers, those that can never be expressed as fractions, were anathemas to the Pythagoreans – they did not fit neatly into their perceived design of the universe. Two particular irrational numbers that have fascinated humankind in its attempt to understand the nature of the world are pi (π) and phi (ϕ), which relate to the circle and the golden section respectively.

Pi is the ratio of the circumference of a circle to its diameter. Its value to eight decimal places is 3.14159265. The ancient Egyptians and the Pythagoreans used the approximation 22/7 (3.14285714….), a convenient rational number, often good enough for practical purposes. Mathematicians have since found methods for calculating pi to any required degree of accuracy using *infinite series*, like the following which was discovered by Leibnitz in 1673:

$$\pi/4 = 1 - 1/3 + 1/5 - 1/7 + 1/9 - 1/11 + 1/13 \ldots \text{etc.}$$

The successive positive and negative terms swing the value respectively above and below $\pi/4$, getting closer and closer the more terms are added. Elegant though it is, hundreds of terms are needed to get an accurate calculation of pi using this particular series.

The *golden section*, also known as the *Divine Proportion*, is a ratio expressing an aesthetically pleasing asymmetry found in nature. It was studied by the Greeks, was probably known to the Ancient Egyptians, is apparent in ancient Celtic art (e.g. in the spirals) and was used to great effect by renaissance artists such as Piero della Francesca (c. 1420-1492 AD). The name 'sectio aurea' has been attributed to Leonardo da Vinci (1452-1519 AD). The golden section can be visualised as a straight line divided into two unequal sections **a** and **b**, representing respectively the smaller and larger sections, such that ratio of the larger to the smaller (**b**/**a**) is equal to the ratio of the sum of both to the larger [(**a**+**b**)/**b**]. This ratio or *golden section* is often denoted by the Greek symbol phi (ϕ). Its value to five decimal places is 1.61803. It can be calculated from the formula: $\phi = (1 + \sqrt{5})/2$.

In his *Liber Abaci* (see page 7), Fibonacci (c. 1170-1250 AD) mentions a series of numbers which describe a particular type of natural growth pattern – Fibonacci numbers. He was working on a hypothetical problem involving population growth in a colony of breeding rabbits. Each new number in the Fibonacci series is the sum of the preceding two numbers. Thus we have:

1, 1, 2, 3, 5, 8, 13, 21, 34, 55, 89, and so on

As the series progresses, the ratio of the last number to the penultimate number converges closer and closer to, but never quite reaches, the value of the golden section, ϕ. Such is the fascination of mathematics – to some at least.

The golden section has mystical associations too. It appears in the structure of the *pentagram* (*pentangle*), the five cornered star revered by the Babylonians, the Pythagoreans and, of course, magicians. The pentagram is constructed from five interlinked and intersecting straight lines of equal length (fig 2.1). A regular pentagon is formed at the centre. The intersections divide the lines in the Divine Proportion.

Fig. 2.1

The Pentagram

In this figure, b/a = (a + b)/b = phi = 1.618....

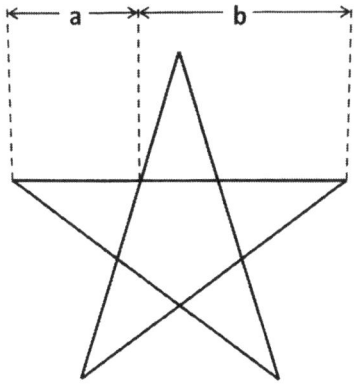

Number Systems

The ancient Egyptians, Indians and Chinese all used forms of the decimal (base 10) system. The use of base 10 is arbitrary and may have originated from counting fingers. In some circumstances other bases are preferable. It has often been customary in our schools to introduce the concept of number bases together with related topics such as roots, powers, indices and logarithms. Perhaps this is one of those points at which many people lose their interest in mathematics. Working with different bases is not difficult – in fact, we do it all the time. The different bases that have been, or still are, used to underpin number systems include 2 (binary or dyadic), 10 (decimal or denary), 12 (duodecimal), 16 (hexadecimal), 20 (vigesimal) and 60 (hexagesimal).

Fragmented forms of a duodecimal system remain as the dozen (12), the gross (144 or 12x12), hours AM and PM, inches in a foot and previously pennies in a shilling. The duodecimal system has some advantages in that it provides more submultiple fractions ($1/_2$, $1/_3$, $1/_4$, $1/_6$, $1/_{12}$) than does the decimal system ($1/_2$, $1/_5$, $1/_{10}$). However, to be as versatile as the decimal system for use in complex calculations it needs specific symbols to replace the decimal numbers 10 and 11. As mentioned previously, an effective number system requires, in addition to a symbol for zero, separate symbols for all numbers less than the base value. In fact, the Duodecimal Society, founded in the USA in the 1940's, championed a more extensive use of a base 12 system that used specific symbols for 10 and 11, namely X and E respectively. It hasn't caught on!

The binary (base 2) system has only two symbols, 0 and 1, the minimum that can be used to represent information. The ancient Chinese were familiar with the binary system. The German philosopher and mathematician Leibnitz (1646-1716 AD), a reputed follower of the Pythagoreans, is usually credited with the introduction of the system in Europe. He was also interested in the mystical properties of numbers – to him, 0 was the void and 1 was God. Binary numbers are rather unwieldy for everyday arithmetic calculations. For instance, the binary number 11011 is equivalent to the decimal number 27. The binary system is of great importance, however, as the mathematical language of logic (0 = false, 1 = true) and as the basis of the binary code, the basic *machine code* of the electronic computer. Binary codes are sequences consisting of 0's and 1's, represented in the computer circuitry by a corresponding series of low ('off') and high ('on') voltage states. The hexadecimal system (base 16) is also used in computing. It uses letters A to F to replace decimal numbers 10 to 15.

The Babylonians used an incomplete hexagesimal system (base 60). But they had specific symbols only for numbers 1 and 10 which were conglomerated together to form the other numbers. The use of 60 is still preserved today in the measurement of minutes and seconds. The Maya used a mainly vigesimal system (base 20) for extensive measurements of time (table 4.1 in chapter 4). They had symbols for zero and for numbers 1 and 5, which were compounded to give hieroglyphics for the other numbers in the system. Large numbers were written in the form of a vertical stack, with the lowest place-value at the bottom and the highest at the top.

Chapter 3
Beliefs about Numbers

Today, mathematics and the sciences of chemistry and astronomy are largely divorced from their esoteric counterparts, numerology, alchemy and astrology. Not that long ago, many of the founders of modern science explored both the empirical and mystical aspects of these subjects, which were seen as part of the wider scheme of things. From ancient times, astronomy, astrology and the study of numbers have been intimately interconnected and used in mankind's attempt to unravel the mysteries of the Universe. Throughout history there have been what might broadly be called the mainstream occultists, claiming to be adepts in the secret wisdom, and the more peripheral and diverse groups practising various trivialised, popularised and often lucrative versions of the arcane. Today we are saturated with the latter. Mainstream occultism may provide some insight into the human predicament, and possibly into the complex, and seemingly strange, workings of the human brain.

Much of what we think we know about ancient mysticism and magic comes from second-hand and sometimes dubious interpretations of obscure texts written hundreds or even thousands of years ago about the beliefs and practices of cults, which in turn may have flourished hundreds or thousands of years earlier still. Thus, we rely on Plato's account of Pythagorean thought and of Atlantis. At different times religious and arcane sects and societies have been variously encouraged, suppressed, persecuted and disbanded. New, sometimes modified, versions have arisen to replace or compete with them. One difficulty is that much of the esoteric knowledge was kept secret, being passed on only by spoken word from master to initiate. Occultists claim knowledge from the *akashic record*. Apparently, this is a *cosmic* record that transcends time and is available to those with special clairvoyant powers. It chronicles, in a non-physical *etheric* plane, all past, present and future human events, thoughts and actions. At this point we do not need to worry too much about the latter, or the Atlanteans, or especially the Lemurians, who according to occult tradition were the extremely ancient and barely human progenitors of the Atlanteans. But one enduring theme underlying many branches of occultism is the idea that in the dim and distant past humankind had awareness of the spiritual world, which it subsequently lost. Apparently, since then, small bands of adepts, who have managed by various means to retain or develop the necessary supersensitive powers, have become the keepers of the secret knowledge. Esotericists, and others, would maintain that occultism, the great eastern religions and many of the traditions and symbolisms of the major western religions had common origins. Occultism tends to have more in common with eastern religions, particularly in beliefs about such things as cosmic cycles and reincarnation.

The Pythagoreans represent an important nodal point in Western esoteric tradition. Pythagoras studied mathematics and astronomy in Babylon, learnt the secrets of ancient Greek mystical religions (such as Orphism) and probably also received occult knowledge from the Indians and the Egyptians. Some believe that he, or his followers, may also have had contact with Celtic Druids in Gaul or possibly Britain. The Pythagoreans integrated the various occult traditions, including secret knowledge of numbers, into their own philosophy. Their school, based in Croton in southern Italy, was initially influential but increasing political involvement eventually led to its violent suppression in the 5th century BC. Plato (c. 427-347 BC) took up and taught the ideas of the Pythagoreans, although the more esoteric aspects were probably passed on by spoken word only. Some five hundred years later, Plotinus (c. 205-270 AD) and others founded the Neo-Platonists, a school of philosophy which combined the ideas of Pythagoras, Plato and Aristotle (384-322 BC – Plato's pupil) and continued the esoteric tradition. The Romans, by then ruling most of the 'civilised' world, were initially fascinated by such arcane doctrines and absorbed them into their own culture. But once Christianity had gained official state recognition rival religious beliefs were discouraged, sometimes violently. The Byzantine emperor Justinian the Great (483-565 AD) proscribed Neo-Platonism. Occultism reappeared in various guises in the second millennium, one important form originating from the kabbalah, an ancient Jewish mystical tradition.

The Pythagoreans worshipped numbers. They believed that numbers (that is integers, or whole numbers) were the spiritual building blocks of the universe from which all else followed, and that the study of arithmetic and geometric relationships could take them closer to perfect knowledge. They were fascinated by the patterns and shapes formed when the individual building blocks (digits) of the numbers were represented by, for instance, an arrangement of pebbles. Thus, the numbers 3, 6 and 10 were regarded as triangular and 4, 9 and 16 were regarded as square (fig. 3.1). The *tetraktys* was particularly venerated. This is the arrangement of ten dots (or pebbles) in the form of a triangle. Its significance lies in the fact that the numbers 1, 2, 3 and 4 (counts of dots) which make up the layers of the triangle add up to ten, which was regarded as the number of perfection.

Fig. 3.1

Triangular and Square Numbers

a. Triangular numbers

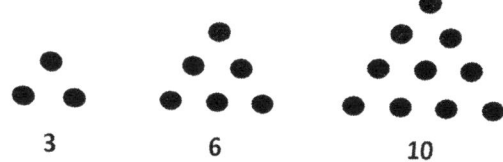

b. Square numbers

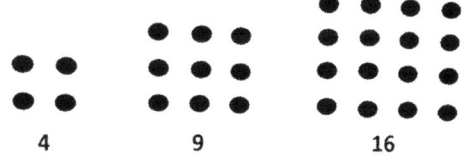

A square number can be built from the two preceding triangular numbers; e.g. 16 = 6 + 10.

The so-called triangular of a number is the sum of all the numbers from one to itself. So, the triangular of 4 is: 1 + 2 + 3 + 4 = 10. There are examples of large triangular numbers in the Bible. For instance, 666 (base 10) is the triangular of 36. The Pythagoreans were also interested in complex three-dimensional geometric figures. They thought the universe could be represented by the dodecahedron, a figure with twelve regular pentagons (plane five-sided figures) covering its surface.

One (i.e. 1) was regarded as a singular metaphysical entity – not really a number. It was that from which all numbers were created and was identified with God. *Two* represented duality, opposition, separation and distance, and was also regarded as the first female number. All odd numbers from *three* onwards were regarded as male, whereas all even numbers were regarded as softer feminine numbers. The numbers *five* (= 2 + 3) and *six* (= 2 x 3) were associated with male-female interactions, such as marriage. In spatiotemporal terms, 1, 2, 3, 4 and 5 could represent position, linear distance, area, volume and time respectively.

The Pythagoreans also studied the relationship between number and musical harmony. They discovered that halving the length of a string (i.e. ratio of 1 to 2) produced appealing harmony – the new note being an octave higher than the original note. They also noted that ratios of 3 to 4 and 2 to 3 produced the harmonious notes known (now) as perfect fourths and perfect fifths respectively. This reinforced their belief in the prime importance of number in cosmological order and harmony.

The ancient, and not so ancient, Chinese also believed that numbers held mysterious powers. A good example is the *magic square* discovered around 2100 BC. It later became the *Lo shu* (pattern of the River Lo) and then consisted of a square of the numbers 1 to 9 in which all rows, columns and diagonals add up to 15 (Fig. 3.2). The numbers are balanced around the central 5.

Fig. 3.2

Lo shu – the Chinese Magic Square

4	9	2
3	5	7
8	1	6

This magic square was later believed to reflect the basic pattern of the universe and was associated with a time mandala called the Later Heaven (also known as the Inner World Arrangement). The numbers 5 and 15 were thought to have special mystical powers. Such numerological relationships influenced Chinese music and architecture, guided societal routine and formed the basis of esoteric practices such as divination.

Numbers were also revered by the ancient Jews. They believed that God used seven letter-numbers as the building blocks of the universe, corresponding to the seven days of creation. Numbers figure prominently in the symbolism of the Bible – both in the Old and New Testaments. For hundreds of years Jewish scholars have searched for possible hidden meanings and messages behind the ancient texts of the Pentateuch (Books of Moses – the first five books of the Old Testament), which form the basis of the Talmud – the definitive exposition of Jewish religious law. One approach involved the numerical analysis of the words and sentences. As mentioned earlier, letters of the Hebrew alphabet can double-up as numbers. Consequently a word could be given a numerical value, and that value could then be converted into a completely different word – a sort of recoding. These techniques were well known in biblical times. Sometimes there was a strong element of mysticism in their use. But they were also used in a more mundane way to convey information covertly – in more dangerous times for instance. Methods included: *isopsephia*, calculating a name from the sum of its letters; *gematria*, relating this to another name or word; and *notarikon*, creating a sentence from each letter in a given word by using them as the first letters of the new words. Well known examples of such trickery are the use of 666 as a code for the Greek form of Nero Caesar (using transliterated Hebrew letters) and 888 as the number of Jesus (using Greek alphabetic-numeral equivalents).

Numerology is the esoteric study of numbers and their supposed effect on human affairs and destiny. Claims that it is a science misrepresent its nature and scope. Forms of numerology were used in many ancient cultures and go back thousands of years. Today's versions are usually based either on the kabbalah using Hebrew letter-numbers or on a Pythagorean system using Greek letter-numbers. Both systems have been simplified and adapted for use with our current alphabet. So-called *life numbers* and *destiny numbers* are calculated from a person's birth date and name respectively. From these and other variations on the theme the numerologist may make interpretations about an individual's personality and tendencies, and suggest how they might favourably lead their life. Some go further and claim that the method has utility for predicting the outcome of football matches and the like. In addition to numerology, New-Age counsellors often practise a variety of related esoteric techniques, such as astrology, palmistry, I Ching and the Tarot. Many people today have little respect for some of these activities, or regard them as forms of psychological manipulation or entertainment. Nevertheless, the high volume of book sales testifies to a widespread and popular interest in these subjects. Even in recent times, people in powerful positions, including some national leaders, have used these methods in planning their activities. Through such channels, numerology and the like can seriously affect all our destinies.

In some cultures and sects the reverence for numbers has been intimately connected with sacred calendars and beliefs about time. This aspect will be covered in Chapter 4. Listing the properties and numerological significances that have been attributed to all the individual numbers would be an unnecessary distraction.

It would be more useful to try to understand the mechanisms and reasons, the how and the why, behind the associations human beings tend to make with particular numbers. These may be related to the nature of the observable physical world, the proclivity of the human mind or brain for particular patterns of association and other more abstract and less easily defined influences. The components of this triad are less discrete and more interconnected than may be apparent at first sight. To explore these ideas further let us use the example of the number *seven*, which assumes considerable importance in *The Revelation of St. John*, the subject of Chapter 5. Consider the following far from exhaustive list of associations and statements:

- seven seas
- seven hills of Rome
- seven wonders of the ancient world
- seven deadly sins
- seven colours of the rainbow
- seven notes of the diatonic scale
- seven days of the week
- seven days of creation (biblical)
- seven globes, rounds and planetary chains (occultism)
- seven seals, trumpets and bowls (Revelation)
- seven psychic centres (occultism)
- seven properties of the physical world (alchemy)
- seven is the number of magic (occultism)
- seven is the number of creation and the cosmos (ancient numerology*)

    * [(4 +3) is the square plus the triangle, representing the world (4) and the supreme deity (3)].

To many of these, one's first reaction might be a resounding "so what"! Some of these associations may seem trivial or arbitrary. Nevertheless, these and other such examples are frequently quoted in religious and esoteric writings as a justification or back-up for a belief in the special power of the number. Superficially, some seem to be no more than a count of particular entities that happen to exist in that number. But it's not that simple. There is a Procrustean tendency at work, an urge to make things conform to a particular pattern or number. Why pick seven man-made wonders of the ancient world? In fact the list varies – so why not have, say, ten. On a good day, seven reasonably distinct colours might be discerned in the rainbow – although picking out indigo between blue and violet can be tricky. The prismatic spectrum is a continuum of light wave frequencies which we arbitrarily divide into discrete colours, partly because our eyes have a particular mixture of colour receptors, our perceptive and cognitive functions interpret the signals in a particular way and our language for expressing what we see is limited. This is reminiscent of the Pythagorean approach to numbers. Some things may be discrete, but often we just prefer to define them that way. *Real* numbers can be represented on a line forming a continuum from zero towards infinity. Both rational numbers and irrational numbers have precise positions on this line, although our system for expressing that position may be imperfect.

The human mind almost certainly has an innate proclivity for certain patterns of association – indeed survival probably depends upon it. Nowadays this might be attributed to the deep structures of the cognitive mechanisms operating in the brain. It is essentially similar to what Freud called "archaic remnants" and Jung called "archetypes". It is a tendency to form particular types of symbolic representation. Jungian psychologists suggest that *four* is a common basis of representation. Thus, in their view, there may be a tendency to categorise in groups of four, or multiples of four, even when no clear division really exists in nature – the four winds, the four seasons, the four cardinal points and so on. The same idea might be applied to certain basic geometric forms, such as squares, rectangles and crosses. Some of these tendencies may become deeply engrained early in life – such as thought and behaviour patterns acquired as part of the cultural heritage. Others may be inborn and present in all of us, perhaps to varying degrees. Carl Jung applied the term 'collective unconscious' to this aspect of the mind. Its primordial brooding nature, instincts and archetypes influence other cognitive functions – sometimes producing unexpected and disturbing results.

In some ancient cultures *four* was regarded as the number of creation and the number of the universe, in particular the natural or physical universe. The Greek philosopher Empedocles (? 490-430 BC) came to the conclusion that the world is composed of the *four elements* Fire, Earth, Air and Water, and that these are governed by the opposing forces of love (or harmony) and strife (or discord). *Four* has prominence in Indian religions. In Hinduism there are the four classes (Varnas), the Four Ends of Man and the four stages of life (Ashramas). In Buddhism there are the four noble truths and the eightfold path.

The origin of the association of *seven* with mystical properties and powers is complicated. There are, of course, the obvious biblical connections, such as the story of the Creation in seven days – but these almost certainly had earlier pagan origins. There is the Babylonian (Chaldean) connection with the seven *'planets'*, the celestial bodies wandering mysteriously across the sky, at least those visible to the Ancients – the sun, the moon, and the proper planets, Saturn, Jupiter, Mars, Venus and Mercury. The Romans adopted these 'planets' as Rulers of the heavens, and as rulers of man's destiny. Occult tradition maintains that cosmic evolution progresses in steps of seven – passing through seven conditions of consciousness (*planetary stages*), each of which passes through seven stages of life (*rounds*), each of which passes through seven conditions of form (*globes*). So, there are 7x7x7 conditions in all. Allegedly, we are in the fourth globe of the fourth round of the fourth planetary (Earth) stage of our evolutionary cycle.

Seven is said to have magic powers and to be associated with the moon. Occultists maintain that magic rituals can only be performed properly at the time of the full moon. Ancient occult and religious tradition considered *seven* to be the sacred number of the Cosmos, the number of completion, because it comprises *four*, representing the creation of the material or natural universe, and *three*, the number of the Divine – the square plus the triangle.

At this point we run into some difficulties of belief about where God fits into the scheme. For some, God, as a single Divine Being, creates the world distinct from himself – the world is dependent on God, but it is not God. For others, God is always part of the cosmos and the continuing cycle of creation and destruction – the divine is the true reality and the world is the illusion our minds perceive of it. Despite the theological differences, *three* has long been a divine number, and still is in the Christian church. The Trinity is the union of the Father, the Son and the Holy Spirit into the one Godhead. There is also a corresponding trinity of evil.

Religious and occult beliefs often allude to a correspondence between the microcosm that is man and the supposed divine structure of the macrocosm. *Genesis* tells us that man is made in the image of God. Esoteric traditions favour motifs of *fours*, *threes* and *sevens* in various combinations. Some talk of the trinity of man as a composite of the physical body, the soul or psychical nature of man and the overshadowing immortal spirit. Others prefer more complex combinations, such as the quarternary of man's basic natures (the physical, astral, etheric and ego) plus the ternary spiritual nature – *four* plus *three*. Some see the cosmos reflected in seven bodily centres of psychic energy, seven *chakras*. The kabbalists superimpose the ten sefiroth of the Tree of Life, the ten spheres of divine emanation corresponding to ten fundamental attributes of God, onto the image of primal man – *Adam Kadmon*. Others might argue that God and the Divine and the numbers and images associated with them are all creations of human cognition – perhaps God in the image of man.

During the last hundred years or so, there has been an increasing tendency for esotericists to latch onto the latest scientific findings, especially in the fields of relativity, quantum physics and cosmology, and to make analogies or parallels with ancient ideas concerning matter, space, time and the forces of nature, and supernature. These sciences are now exploring areas dogged by uncertainty – they operate at the frontiers of human knowledge and at the limits of technical capability. The boundary between physics and metaphysics is becoming increasingly indistinct. Nevertheless, however limited scientific tools may be in unravelling the ultimate mysteries of the universe, scientists will still prefer evidence to superstition. The science at these frontiers is difficult, even for scientists, and it is often misunderstood and misinterpreted by people without the necessary academic background and scientific training. Not surprisingly, many of the analogies, parallels and correlations drawn with mysticism are crude and superficial. But some are tantalising, pointing to interesting alternative paradigmatic approaches (as exemplified in Fritjof Capra's 'The Tao of Physics'). New discoveries about the nature of the universe and the mathematical laws describing it appear to take us closer to an understanding of the grand design and the processes of creation and decay – perhaps forever moving closer but never reaching that elusive, perhaps increasingly illusive, final answer.

Chapter 4
The Numbers of Time

The nature of time, and related topics, such as the age of the world, attract a variety of opinions. Often, views are influenced more by belief than by evidence.

Concepts of Time

Astrophysicists now think that the Universe, and time, started with a *big bang* at a single point (a *singularity*) about 14 billion years ago. It then expanded and developed into the form that exists today. Apparently, current evidence also suggests that it will continue to expand, possibly even sprouting parallel universes. The Abrahamic religions assume that, for our world, time had a definite beginning and will proceed towards a definite end. Some belief systems assume that time has a more continuous cyclical nature, with the end of one cycle passing on to the beginning of the next.

Physicists, cosmologists, philosophers and psychologists still ponder, and argue, over the concept of time. Like consciousness, it has an abstract quality. In practical terms, time amounts to the passing of events, one after the other. In everyday life, we use clocks and calendars to schedule and log events. Physicists tell us that the Newtonian concept of time, as a straightforward linear entity, breaks down under the extreme conditions in which time and space are *warped*. Such conditions include close proximity to black holes and intense gravitational fields. Back on Earth, thankfully, Newtonian physics appears to work very well for the day-to-day, and year-to-year, activities of us ordinary mortals.

Before the advent of timing devices, ancient humans related the occurrence, and concurrence, of important events to recurring natural phenomena, such as the lunar and solar cycles, the seasons, and days. The lengths of these natural cycles can vary. Today we calibrate our clocks and watches against standard times, such as Greenwich Mean Time (GMT). A *tomic clocks* now provide the very accurate stable reference values. The SI unit of time is the *second*. Put in simple terms (!), it is now defined as the duration of 9,192,631,770 transitions of particular electron orbitals in the caesium-133 atom. The *hour* is still 3,600 seconds (in the 'equal hours' system).

Dates and Calendars

The solar year (tropical year) is the time taken for the Earth to make one rotation around the Sun. Its average value is approximately 365 days 5 hours 49 minutes – but it can vary up or down by a few minutes each year. The Romans introduced their Julian Calendar in 46 BC. This included a leap year of 366 days every four years in order to adjust for the error that would otherwise occur if all years were measured only as 365 days. It aimed to ensure that the astronomical and calendrical estimates of the vernal equinox would continue to correlate well into the future. But, after many centuries a significant gap of several days had developed. The Gregorian Calendar (Pope Gregory XIII), that we still use today, was introduced in 1582 AD. Apart from a one-off readjustment, it introduced slight modifications to the Julian Calendar that would ensure even greater accuracy in future years. Leap years are now omitted for all years divisible by 100, except those divisible by 400. So, 1900 AD was not a leap year, but 2000 AD was.

The Anno Domini (AD) reference was invented by Dionysius Exiguus, a 6th century monk and scholar. Its popularity spread following its use in the historical works of the Venerable Bede, an 8th century English monk (canonised to St Bede in the 19th century). The Gregorian Calendar uses the birth of Jesus Christ as the reference point, giving rise to years BC (Before Christ) and AD. 1 AD follows immediately after 1 BC. There is no year 0! In this scheme, Jesus Christ was born in the year 1 AD. However, many biblical scholars have argued that the actual date of Christ's birth was a few years earlier, around 4 BC on the Gregorian Calendar. Some of the prophecies for the dates of doomsday may not have taken these factors into account. The 'Common Era' notation is sometimes preferred to the use of BC and AD because it avoids a specific religious association. Thus, BCE (Before Common Era) and CE (Common Era) can be used in place of BC and AD respectively.

There are several other important calendrical systems. Some are very ancient, such as the Egyptian calendar which dates back some five millennia. These often involved complex divisions of the lunisolar cycles and took account of both practical functional (e.g. farming) and religious requirements. Some systems have complex cyclical structures involving millions, even billions, of years.

The rediscovery, decoding and interpretation of the Mayan calendar in recent times illustrates some of the difficulties encountered in this field of archaeology. Mayan astronomy and mathematics were at an advanced stage in the early centuries AD. Their observations on solar and lunar cycles, and on the movement of other heavenly bodies, especially the planet Venus, were used to construct a complex calendrical system. Many of the original records of Mayan observations and culture were burnt by Christian zealots following the European invasions of Mesoamerica in the 16th century. Thanks to a few enlightened scholars, some accounts of the Mayan civilisation are still available. Fortunately, the Maya also recorded key facts about historical and religious events, and their numerical and calendrical systems, on stone structures which have survived the test of time. Of particular importance is the Great Lid of Palenque, rediscovered less than a century ago. This is a huge rectangular solid stone lid that still covers a tomb in a monumental pyramidal building known as the Temple of Inscriptions.

From such sources of information, the Mayan number system has been accurately decoded. It is a vigesimal (base 20) system, which was slightly modified for the measurement of time (table 4.1).

Table 4.1

The Mayan Modified Vigesimal (Base 20) System for the Measurement of Time

Starting with the *kin*, a day, it proceeds as follows:

1 uinal	= 20 kin	
1 tun	= 18 uinal	= 360 days
1 katun	= 20 tun	= 7,200 days
1 baktun	= 20 katun	= 144,000 days
1 piktun	= 20 baktun	= 2,880,000 days
1 kalabtun	= 20 piktun	= 57,600,000 days

(the series continues, using base 20).

The Mayan calendar was probably based on a system used by their predecessors, the Olmec, many centuries BC. It involved different types of year and a complex system of names and numbers for the identification of individual days. But for historical dating and future forecasting the Maya developed a separate system known as the *long count*. This is a continuous linear count of days extending over thousands of years. It is divided into the so-called *great cycles*, each of which lasts 13 baktuns.

So,	1 great cycle	= 13 baktuns
		= 13 x 144,000 days
		= 1,872,000 days
		= 5,125 years

Myanologists have been able to correlate the Mayan *long count* with the Gregorian calendar. Apparently, the last *great cycle* started in 3114 BC and ended in 2012 AD. Prior to this latter date, modern prophets of doom were, of course, predicting cataclysmic events for the end of that cycle. As far as I know, nothing particularly apocalyptic occurred in 2012. Ironically, descendants of the Maya, still living in parts of Mesoamerica, celebrated the passing of the last *great cycle* and welcomed the beginning of the current *great cycle*.

Chapter 5
The Revelation of St. John

Revelation is the last book of the Holy Bible and it purports to unveil God's plan for humankind.

The old aphorism *'not seeing the wood for the trees'* is doubly apt when applied to the study of Revelation. In this case the trees themselves are indistinct, often allegorical, symbolic or parodic. They are planted in a bizarre and illusory landscape that defies dimensional perception. The *trees* give clues to the *wood* and the *wood* gives clues to the *trees*. But which clues are important and where do we start? An open mind is required – and also a roaming, but not unbridled, imagination.

Taken at face value the Revelation of St. John is repugnant, vindictive and violent – a veritable *coup de grâce* with the element of mercy removed. Its sentiments would not be out of place in the Old Testament, but it appears to be the most *unchristian* book of the New Testament. It provides rich fuel indeed for *hell-fire and damnation* preaching. To paraphrase DH Lawrence – whose last work was entitled '*Apocalypse*' – the previously kind and forgiving Lamb (Christ) now slays mankind by the million. To Christians of a nervous and superstitious disposition, Revelation must have been terrifying. Perhaps it had to be to get the message home against the odds. But, is there still an important message for us today – and if so, what is it? To answer this question with any sort of credibility requires consideration not only of the textual details but also the origin and nature of the material and the circumstances in which it was written. This is easier said than done.

Essential Background

Over the centuries, hundreds of works have been produced on this subject, by all sorts, including scholars, mystics, zealots and lunatics. One thing is for sure, the Apocalypse of St. John can be interpreted in many different ways – and in almost every respect it still remains an enigma.

Even its authorship is uncertain. Some scholars see the hands of several authors, while others (e.g. the respected theologians Swete and Sweet) sensed a single mind behind the whole work. Lawrence thought it a "second rate mind" – strange might be a better description. The two main contenders were both called John. One is John the Apostle, son of Zebedee, who was also assumed to be the author of the fourth Gospel and some of the Epistles of the New Testament. The other is John the Elder, of whom less is known. He was a disciple of Jesus but not an apostle. Attribution revolves around such things as dates, ages, travels, status and the views of early writers – none of these are particularly reliable – and on literary style and content. The puzzle may never be solved. All that can be said is that a person called John, while residing on the Aegean island of Patmos, possibly in exile, claimed to have written Revelation following divine vision and audition. This John of Patmos was probably a Jewish Christian of high standing in the church of Asia Minor. The author had an extensive knowledge and deep understanding of the Old Testament and almost certainly of pagan and occult traditions too.

Revelation was probably first 'published' in the last third of the 1st century. A more precise date would be useful in understanding the need for, and purpose of, this missive in a local historical context. Modern scholars tend to favour a date around 95 AD, although some have argued for an earlier date of around 68 AD, at the end of Nero's reign (54-68 AD). Christians had suffered the most horrid tortures and deaths under Nero. They may have been better tolerated during Domitian's reign (81-96 AD), despite a late period of terror, provided they kept their religion to themselves and did not indulge in overt *witness-bearing*. One theory is that many Christians were then becoming more complacent or compromising in their faith and were beginning to accept the authority and mores of the Roman State (Sweet) – no doubt a safer option. They needed to be reminded of the previous holocaust and of dangers still ahead, particularly those threatening the survival of the church itself.

The definitive and authoritative list of Holy Scriptures, the canon, was finalised in the 4th century. Much material was excluded, particularly that of doubtful or non-apostolic origin. Revelation was included – although some parts of the church were very much against it. John's original Greek manuscripts are not available, so we rely on the accuracy of later transcriptions and their translations. Scribes may have modified or rearranged the text in later editions. But the spooky warning, a well-known trick of the trade, at the end of Revelation might have prevented some tampering.

"I warn every one who hears the words of the prophecy of this book: if any one adds to them, God will add to him the plagues described in this book, and if any one takes away from the words of the book of this prophecy, God will take away his share in the tree of life and in the holy city, which are described in this book." (Revelation $22^{18,19}$, Revised Standard Version).

In some recent versions of the Bible attempts have been made to simplify the text and to interpret some of the cryptic passages to make the going easier and more meaningful for the modern reader. In so doing, hidden meanings may have become further obscured.

Revelation is typical of the Jewish apocalyptic genre epitomised by the Book of Daniel in the Old Testament. In its structure, content and symbolism Revelation borrows heavily from Daniel and Ezekiel. It may also be taken as a reiteration of Christ's vaguer apocalyptic warning given on the Mount of Olives. On their first exposure, the modern reader is likely to find the book utterly confusing. It was written to be read to a different audience, in different times and in a very different setting. That audience may have been more used to this seemingly strange style of presentation, and to the allegory and symbolism which dominates the book. There are numerous astrological references. Its effect was meant to be dramatic. The subject matter is structured and reiterated in a way more akin to a symphony than a work of literature – bizarre motifs appear and reappear in various guises, and there are unexpected liturgical interludes and asides, but the main themes steadily develop with extensive use of symbolism and parody. Revelation is complex and much of its symbolism has not been convincingly explained. It is rich ground indeed for the exegete, whose imagination, especially in the absence of scholastic discipline, is in danger of running wild.

The first three chapters of Revelation concern letters which John claimed he was commanded by the *'son of man'* (Christ) to write to the *seven* churches of Asia Minor, which may have represented symbolically the *whole* of Christianity. The seven letters warn the churches to guard against the dangers of complacency, compromise with the prevailing mores of society and the infiltration of heathen morals and practices. The bulkier central section contains the plan for the world, including the prophecies of beastly and supernatural things, which are unveiled by the *seven* seals, heralded by the *seven* trumpets and finally poured from the *seven* bowls of wrath. The gist of Revelation, or at least its face-value message to the Christian congregations, might be summarised briefly as follows. Christ's heavenly revelation to John warns that not all is well on the Earth (not much has changed then!) and that, despite the difficulties ahead, the faithful must not flag in their witness to God. It foretells of devastating natural and supernatural disasters, of battles in Heaven and on Earth between God's team and Satan's team, and of the imminent end of the world, or at least the prevailing world order. But Jesus is coming again soon. Although they may have to suffer in the short-term, God's loyal and faithful subjects will be protected and will eventually find happiness in paradise. The souls of the dead martyrs call for vengeance. Their persecutors, or their persecutors' souls, and the faithless and disloyal, will suffer unmerciful torment – if possible, worse than that suffered by the martyrs themselves. The sentiment is captured by a characteristic outburst near the end of the book:

"But as for the cowardly, the faithless, the polluted, as for murderers, fornicators, sorcerers, idolators, and all liars, their lot shall be in the lake that burns with fire and brimstone, which is the second death." (Revelation 21^8, Revised Standard Version).

Was John's Revelation really divine? Many Christian fundamentalists believe that it was. Some modern Christian scholars are coy on the matter, some preferring to talk vaguely in terms of Jungian psychology, the *collective unconscious*, and an altered mental state associated with deep meditation. Theosophists claim that Revelation describes an esoteric Christian initiation experience, one associated with an altered state of consciousness and clairvoyance. The fact that Revelation is fantastical, includes a kaleidoscope of ideas and bits and pieces taken from the Old Testament and other ancient sources, and on the surface smacks of the sort of vengeful zealotry so often found in radical religious sects, then and now, does not negate the possibility of some sort of divine intervention. After all, who or whatever was behind it, the message had to be translated into a form that humankind could understand – not just in John's time but throughout human history. Its effect had to be powerful enough to ensure not only its own survival but that of Christianity. At least, we might reasonably assume that John, whoever he was, believed in his vision.

Different levels of interpretation can often be applied to particular entities and symbols, such as the enigmatic rider of the white horse, or to broader scenes such as the opening of the seven seals or the whole triple heptad of seals, trumpets and bowls. There may be a limited Christian message seemingly focused on local contemporary events, but underneath this, or interpreted another way, there may be a broader message that still has relevance today. Perhaps there may be an allusion to a more profound and universal meaning, something that might be of great importance to humankind as a whole, perhaps pointing to cataclysmic events that are almost inevitable in the course of human evolution. Most of the numbers and time periods mentioned in Revelation (e.g. the binding of Satan in the pit for a thousand years – the millennium) are probably meant to be interpreted symbolically rather than literally. Nevertheless, such statements have provided exegetes with endless years of distraction and speculation concerning possible dates for doomsday.

There may well be truly *occult* messages hidden within the body of this New Testament document, just as some viruses hide within and usurp the mechanisms of host cells to meet their own ends, waiting for their messages to be translated, transcribed and spread at some future date. Whether such hidden messages, those that are not the figments of over-imaginative exegesis, are of divine origin or inspiration or are just the machinations of an obsessional or deluded ancient human brain is a matter of interpretation or belief.

Seals, Trumpets and Bowls

The scene is set in Heaven where the '*One*' (God – the Creator) is surrounded by worshipping creatures and elders. He holds a scroll sealed with seven seals – it contains his will for the world. The Lamb (Christ), still bearing the marks of slaughter, has won through his sacrifice the right to open the seals. The Lamb is depicted with seven horns and seven eyes, "*which are the seven spirits of God sent out into all the earth*". Conventionally, the horns and eyes are taken to symbolise power and wisdom. Even before the opening of the first seal the text contains a profusion of astrological and numerological symbols, ensuring a proliferation of divergent interpretations.

The prophecies of death and destruction are contained in the seals, trumpets and bowls sections. The opening of the seals reveals the birth-pangs of the new age, as already foretold by Jesus.

> *"…. but the end is still to come. For nation will make war upon nation, kingdom upon kingdom; there will be famines and earthquakes in many places. With all these things the birth-pangs of the new age begin."* [Matthew $24^{7,\ 8}$; New English Bible]

The messages in the seals section are recapitulated and expanded in the trumpet and bowls sections. Using a crude modern business analogy the seals section might be said to contain the mission statement, a hint of strategy and the overall plan. The executive plan is then spelled out in increasingly gory detail in the trumpets and bowls sections. Time as we perceive it has little meaning in Heaven, so the scheduling of events is somewhat indeterminate.

On a standard view, the content of the seals, trumpets and bowls sections might be summarised as follows.

The seven seals

1 to 4   the infamous horsemen of the Apocalypse ride out with portents of war, famine, pestilence and death affecting a quarter of mankind – probably brought about by man's own actions

5	the souls of dead martyrs cry out for vengeance
6	a brief preview of what is in store for the earth and mankind – the wrath of the Lamb
7	silence in Heaven for *"about half an hour"*, leading on to the trumpet-blowing angels

The seven trumpets

1 to 4	herald destruction of a third of mankind's natural resources (vegetable and marine life, light, poisoning of fresh water), ostensibly instigated by supernatural forces
5 & 6	herald the first and second *woes*, particularly nasty demonic forces which attack and torment mankind
7	eventually, after a number of highly symbolic interludes, this leads to the third *woe* – the arrival of the devil and its forms on earth and their effects on mankind

The seven bowls of wrath

| 1 to 4 | horrid supernatural attacks affecting all marine life and all people bearing the mark of the beast (i.e. the unfaithful) |
| 5 to 7 | supernatural attack on the beast and its kingdom |

Thus the drama unfolds in a series of sevens. Within each heptad there is a 4, 3, 7 motif, symbolising the material or natural world, the divine or supernatural and the whole respectively (i.e. $4 + 3 = 7$). The revelations of the first four seals, trumpets and bowls are aimed at the earth and the earth dwellers, whereas the last three scenes in each of the series are largely divine or strongly supernatural.

Anthroposophists (Steiner) and other schools of occultism believe that the heptads, and the seals section in particular, contain within them an important occult message, albeit dressed up in Jewish-Christian embellishments. On the other hand, some Christian theologians find an unfortunate element of paganism in what they believe is predominantly an exoteric Christian message. Some scholars feel that the second half of Revelation, most of that following the trumpets section, has a different quality, or is largely a cumbersome addition. Sweet discerns a more complex unifying architecture involving the whole of Revelation, such that the initial impression might be turned on its head. Thus, a seemingly chaotic and repulsive work becomes one of beauty, and perhaps the Lamb is not so unforgiving after all.

This is a convenient point at which to introduce a widely held esoteric interpretation of the opening of the seven seals – an interpretation which will require further elaboration in later sections. On this view the sevenfold nature of man is represented as follows:

physical
etheric – that containing the life energy
astral – the vehicle of sense and emotion
'I' or 'ego'
spirit-self (Manas) – transformed astral
life-spirit (Bhuddi) – transformed etheric
spirit-man (Atma) – transformed physical

The conventional exoteric Christian terms approximating to these entities are the flesh or body for the physical, the soul for a combination of the etheric, astral and the 'I' and the spirit for the remaining three. In occult tradition man is not yet fully developed spiritually and has so far only reached the fifth stage, that involving spiritualisation of the astral body. Apparently, in modern man the astral body is involved with the sensory and emotional world but it has lost its previously held super-sensory powers, which must now be restored. The fourth of these natures, the 'I' or 'ego' (not synonymous with the ego of psychology), is our ability to say "I am" with full consciousness. With this type of intelligence, or ego-consciousness, comes the power to choose the path to higher spiritual development, or to ignore it or become besotted by man's recently developed intellect and love of materialism and effectively sink into the *abyss*. Man in general has yet to rise to these higher spiritual planes, although some initiates claim this ability already. The opening of the seals is interpreted as symbolising the first stage of the esoteric Christian initiation during which man's potential in the present epoch and possible development in the next is realised. In this system the seven seals represent the seven cultural stages of our epoch, an epoch concerned with the development of human intelligence. The 'I-am' has been called the 'Christ-principle' – it is the vehicle for the reincarnation of consciousness. Christ has shown mankind the way – mankind with its new found consciousness must now choose.

So, the first four seals represent the first four natures in terms of the development of the intellect. Some will stop at this stage, and will eventually suffer for it. Others will progressively spiritualise their astral, etheric and physical natures such that these will no longer burden them. The opening of the seventh seal symbolises death and rebirth, that is reincarnation, with the freed spiritual 'I' ready for further development in the next epoch. On this view, the key contents of Revelation arose from a higher state of consciousness, a state achieved through an initiation of the sort practised in the ancient pagan Mysteries (Steiner).

Confusing and far-fetched as some of this must seem, there are nevertheless some parallels to modern exoteric theological thought. The synthesis of a new order involves the deconstruction, changing or discarding of the old system – the result is a period of conflict and chaos – the birth pangs of the new age. The faithful, those that follow the *right* spiritual path will benefit, eventually. Those who choose not to follow this path and deny God, or worship false gods, or idolise their intelligence and the material world around them, will not share in the future spiritual fulfilment of mankind, unless they repent in time. Sweet observes, 'that which is not God, if worshipped, becomes a demonic power'. Man brings wrath upon himself by his own thoughts and actions. From either stance this can be seen as the battle for, and the battle within, man's mind – the *abyss* constituting its darkest recess.

The Four Horsemen

The first four unsealings of the scroll release in turn visions of the white, red, black and pale horses. The following abbreviated extracts (6^{2-8}; Revised Standard Version) reveal the nature and portent of the riders.

The white horse

'. . and its rider had a bow; and a crown was given to him, and he went conquering and to conquer.'

The red horse ('bright red')

'. . its rider was permitted to take peace from the earth, so that men would slay one another; and he was given a great sword.'

The black horse

'. . and its rider had a balance in his hand; and I heard what seemed to be a voice in the midst of the four living creatures [four pagan creatures by God's throne in Heaven] saying, "A quart of wheat for a denarius [a penny – a day's wage], and three quarts of barley for a denarius; but do not harm oil or wine!".

The pale horse

'. . and its rider's name was Death, and Hades followed him; and they were given power over a fourth of the Earth, to kill with sword and with famine and with pestilence and by the wild beasts of the earth.'

A simple direct interpretation suggests that, whoever he is, the rider of the white horse is the instigator of change – the start of the trouble. The red horse and its rider represent the war and bloodshed that will arise as a consequence. The third rider represents a degree of famine – the balance is an Old Testament symbol – the diet is limited. The end result is portrayed by the rider whose name is Death – a quarter of mankind to be killed by war, famine, pestilence etc. Within these passages are allusions to contemporary catastrophic events which would have been well known to those living in Asia Minor in the 1st century – and Christians would have been aware of similar accounts in the Old Testament.

The congregations in these times *heard* the story of Revelation; most would not have been able to *read* it. The message in the narration was reinforced in the listener's memory by allusion to the real dramas of the dangerous world in which they lived. The familiar cycle of war followed by famine, infectious disease and death has occurred regularly throughout recorded human history. It is never far away.

Nowadays, we love to hate the gothic horror of the pale horse and its rider, the fourth horseman, whose name is Death. But the rider of the white horse is also sinister, and more enigmatic. He rides out on the opening of the very first seal and seems to be the originator of all that follows. But who, or what, is he? He may hold the key to Revelation. He is already conquering. The white horse and the crown may symbolise righteousness and victory. He could be Christ, or a parody, the Antichrist. Sweet makes a good case for the Christian witness. Is he the 'ego-consciousness' of *righteous* man? Whichever, the bow must surely represent the primary weapon of conquest – communication of the *word*, which itself is a two-edged sword. It is the power of information and propaganda that conquers man's mind and leads to conflict. Note Christ's charge to his disciples:

'You must not think that I have come to bring peace to the earth; I have not come to bring peace, but a sword. I have come to set a man

against his father, a daughter against her mother, a son's wife against his mother-in-law; and a man will find his enemies under his own roof.' [Matthew 10[34-36]; New English Bible].

Enter the red horse and its rider with a big sword, to take peace from the Earth.

The horse has long been a symbol of *intelligence*. From the anthroposophical perspective, the opening of the first four seals represents aspects of the development of human intelligence. According to Steiner, the white horse symbolises spiritualised intelligence, the 'I' entering a new cycle of cosmic development. The red horse indicates that which must be discarded in order to progress – the destructive aspect and the inner strife. Ravenscroft and Wallace-Murphy argue that the white horse refers to the age of clairvoyant-clairaudiant man, man without individual consciousness (apparently ending about 4000 BC); the red horse symbolises the age of individual intelligence, self-conscious thinking and development of deductive logic; the black horse represents the dawn of [modern] science and materialism and the age of inductive reasoning; the pale horse denotes demonic thinking, the age of technical horror, as epitomised by atomic bomb science.

The more specific the interpretation the more we move from symbolism to allegory. At their deepest levels the esoteric and exoteric messages are not that dissimilar. Intelligence and the power to communicate, and thereby influence minds and actions, are the great forces at work in the human world, and they are continually evolving. What might current developments in artificial intelligence and internet technology lead to?

The elevation of a *chosen* group to a better or more advantageous state requires the discarding of that which hinders their progress. But who is *right* or *righteous*? Political propagandists and religious crusaders claim *right* for their sides, whether they are the rulers or the ruled, the suppressors or the suppressed. Revelation champions Christianity. However, whether the rider of the white horse represents Christ, the Antichrist, or the witness of the one or the other, there remains, intentionally or not, a universally applicable message about the power of the *word* and the information battle and its consequences for humankind. It is potently Darwinian – pure evolution.

An Anthroposophical Perspective

A discussion of the seals, trumpets and bowls would not be complete without further consideration of Steiner's anthroposophical interpretation in terms of cosmic evolution. Although this may seem to stretch credulity to the limit, it says much for human ingenuity and, perhaps, the wonders of clairvoyance.

From an early age, Rudolf Steiner (1861–1925 AD) developed his views on intuitive thinking and spirituality. His interests included philosophy, occultism, theosophy, architecture, writing and alternative approaches to education, medicine and agriculture. He played an active role in the Theosophical Society, founded in 1875 by Helena Blavatsky (1831-1891 AD). Unhappy with the later direction of that society, Steiner founded the Anthroposophical Society in 1913. Although both societies had many common positions on spirituality, science and cosmic evolution, he felt that the Theosophical Society was becoming too heavily orientated towards Eastern religion. Steiner claimed clairvoyant powers and the ability to access the mystical *akashic record* (page 17). He had a considerable influence on 20th century esoteric and New-Age thought.

Steiner took a particular interest in 'The Apocalypse of St John'. His scheme of cosmic evolution is quite complex and its intricacies and nuances can be difficult to grasp without detailed study. The following brief account aims to provide a rough guide.

Apparently, the entities that form the cosmos at any particular point have evolved, and will continue to evolve, through several series of conditions and stages, all governed by the number *seven*. From time to time entities falter in their advancement, so that at any particular stage in cosmic evolution there will be present a spectrum of things, beings *et cetera* at different stages of development. Thus, at our stage there are the lesser developed, such as the animals, which lack the 'I', and the plants, which lack the 'I' and the astral component. There are also more advanced forms beyond our normal sensory appreciation. Allegedly, they are represented symbolically in John's vision of the 24 Elders surrounding God's throne. Clairvoyant powers have enabled man to perceive five such series of seven conditions and stages, and all must be passed though successfully to achieve the ultimate spiritual evolution. Steiner tells us that altogether there are 7x7x7x7x7 (i.e. 16,807) conditions. The grandest group, that through which things pass the slowest, comprises the *seven* stages of consciousness. The latter are also called the planetary conditions or chains, and they are given the names Saturn, Moon, Sun, Earth, Jupiter, Venus and Vulcan (*sic*). The reader should appreciate that these are essentially metaphorical titles in that they do not equate to the material *planets* of man's present sense world. We have already passed through the Saturn, Moon and Sun conditions and are now in the Earth condition of consciousness. Next, a very long time in the future, we will enter the Jupiter condition. Before this can happen a subset of conditions must be fulfilled, and before this another sub-subset and so on. In sequence, working down from the Planetary conditions we have:

7 Consciousness conditions (or *Planets*)
7 Life conditions (or *Rounds*)
7 Form conditions (or *Globes*)
7 Epochs
7 Ages (ages of culture or civilisation)

At present, humankind is said to be in the fourth Planet, fourth Round, fourth Globe, fifth Epoch and fifth Age of civilisation. So, in terms of a numerical series our present location in the scheme is:

$$4 - 4 - 4 - 5 - 5$$

The fourth Epoch was the Atlantean – it ended with the so-called Great Flood. Humankind as we know it arose mainly from the survivors of the fifth Atlantean age – our 'root race'. Our Epoch started with the Great Flood. Its first four ages, the ages of civilisation preceding our own, are given as follows:

1st   Ancient Indian
2nd   Ancient Persian
3rd   Babylonian-Chaldean-Egyptian-Hebrew
4th   Graeco-Roman

The Ages are concerned with the development of human intelligence. Only a vestige of the previous rapport with the spiritual world remained as modern man's progenitor passed from the Atlantean Epoch to the first stage of our present Epoch. At its seventh stage the fifth Epoch, our Epoch, will end with the War of All against All – global devastation caused by man's egoism.

In this interpretation, the seven seals symbolise what is sealed into man's soul during this Epoch and the nature of the seven consecutive civilisations of the next. The seven trumpets symbolise the seven stages of the seventh Epoch, which will take us to the boundary of our physical Earth development. The seven bowls of wrath symbolise the expulsion of our material nature at the end of the seventh Epoch, the discarding of that which hinders progression to the highest spiritual level.

In a nutshell, the bowls symbolise the point of divergence where the faithful followers will take on a higher evolutionary form and the non-believers and idolators who refuse to change will be left behind, imprisoned and plagued by their primitive natures.

Chapter 6
Sixes and Sevens

Revelation describes the satanic trinity, which parodies the Holy Trinity.

Holy Trinity	**Satanic Trinity**
The Father	Satan – the great red dragon
The Son	First Beast – the beast from the sea
The Holy Spirit	Second Beast – the beast from the earth

Many of the attributes given to these satanic creatures have been borrowed from the Old Testament and other ancient sources. The first and second beasts bear resemblances to Leviathan and Behemoth. Care must be taken not to make over-rigid comparisons. John's aim here was probably to provide a strong but familiar descriptive or symbolic base upon which additional contemporary messages could be tagged. The great red dragon is synonymous with the serpent, the Devil, Satan and 'the deceiver of the whole world'. He has seven heads and ten horns. The first beast, the beast from the sea (*abyss*), symbolises the Antichrist. It is in the image of Satan and is given the authority and power of Satan on the Earth. The second beast persuades people to worship the first beast – it is a false prophet.

There is little doubt that the satanic trilogy in Revelation is, at one level, an allegorical reference to Rome, its deified Emperors and its advocates. Both Caligula (emperor 37-41 AD) and Nero (emperor 54-68 AD) have attracted the designation of Antichrist.

The number of the beast can be construed simply as a code for a particular Roman emperor, notably Nero. But this is a relatively recent assumption. Early on, it had been thought to represent a person, but the identity of the subject has been a matter of conjecture and uncertainty since the 2nd century. The question of the meaning of 666 in Revelation has not been satisfactorily settled – it is still shrouded in mystery. There are differences in the translations and interpretations of the relevant ancient texts.

The Revised Standard Version (1952) of the Bible provides good modern scholarship without unjustified attempts to *improve* meaning. Its version of Revelation 13[16-18] is given below.

> [16] *Also it [*] causes all . . . . . . to be marked on the right hand or forehead,* [17] *so that no one can buy or sell unless he has the mark, that is, the name of the beast [**] or the number of its name.* [18] *This calls for wisdom: let him who has understanding reckon the number of the beast, for it is a human number, its number is six hundred and sixty-six. [Note: * = second beast; ** = first beast].*

Now compare the much earlier King James version of verse 18:

> 'Here is wisdom. Let him that hath understanding count the number of the beast: for it is the number of a man; and his number is Six hundred three score and six.'

And the Gideon Bible:

> 'If anyone has insight, let him calculate the number of the beast, for it is man's number. The number is 666.'

And the New English Bible:

> ^{18} (Here is the key; and anyone who has intelligence may work out the number of the beast. The number represents a man's name, and the numerical value of its letters is six hundred and sixty-six.)'

There is some ambiguity in the meaning of 'human number', 'number of a man' etc. It could mean a number that is intelligible to mankind, a number that relates to mankind or a number representing a particular person. Christian scholars are not unanimous in their views. The New English Bible has clearly plumped for the last of these options – it offers verse 18 as a more specific note in parentheses. The text of verse 17 lends weight to the idea that the number may represent a person in authority, such as an emperor. But would it have required much intellect, insight and wisdom to have decoded the number in John's time? Surely, it was more obvious then, if not since. Given the partiality for multiple meanings in Revelation, there is a possibility that 666 was intended to be interpreted in different ways – there may be both superficial and *deep* meanings.

The early Greek manuscripts presented the numbers in the form of three letters of the Greek alphabet:

	chi	xi	zeta	
=	600	60	6	(= 666)

As noted in chapter 2, the Greeks and Jews used letters for numbers as well as words. There was an alternative version circulating in the early Christian Church – this gave 616:

	chi	iota	zeta	
=	600	10	6	(= 616)

Although the 666 version is favoured, the possibility of alternative readings does provide some support for the 'Nero Caesar' hypothesis. Transliteration of the Greek form Neron Kaiser into Hebrew letters gives the number equivalent 666. A similar treatment of the Roman form of the name gives the number equivalent 616. Many other people, and even organisations, have been linked conveniently in this way to the number, and therefore the antichrist – usually in the interest of partisan causes. The Nero-Caesar hypothesis fits neatly with the evidence available. However, many exegetes believe that 666 represents more than just a simple code for a particular person's name.

The number can be found in the Old Testament. For instance, in I Kings 10[14] there is a comment that the amount of gold that came to Solomon each year amounted to 666 talents. In occult tradition, gold is the metal of the Sun God. The so-called Sun Magic Square (Fig. 6.1), published by Agrippa in the 16th century, contains all numbers from 1 to 36 arranged in a 6 x 6 pattern, such that each line, column and diagonal add up to 111. The grand total of all the numbers is 666 – i.e., the triangular of 36.

Fig. 6.1

The 6x6 Magic Square of the Sun

6	32	3	34	35	1
7	11	27	28	8	30
19	14	16	15	23	24
18	20	22	21	17	13
25	29	10	9	26	12
36	5	33	4	2	31

Occultists sometimes allude to such associations occurring in more ancient cultures (e.g. Babylonian, Egyptian), but provenance appears less reliable.

One popular idea is that 666 denotes the imperfection of the antichrist because each of its digits falls one short of those in 777

– seven being the number of completeness in a numerological sense. Others have regarded 6 as a perfect number because it is both the sum and the product of its factors (1+2+3 = 6; 1x2x3 = 6). Steiner thought that 666 could be read as the evolutionary number 6-6-6, referring to the point far in the future when the beast and its followers will fall into the abyss, the point of no return. He also claimed that by using ancient mystical (but probably not very *standard*) operating procedures, 666 could be broken down to 400+200+6+60 and then converted to the equivalent Hebrew letters Tav-Resh-Vav-Samek (table 2.1). In sound these letters are said to have occult associations with the first four of the seven natures of man. Further, when read from right to left with vowels inserted they apparently give "Soreth", the Sun demon, which Steiner equated with the second beast – the two-horned beast from the earth. Ravenscroft and Wallace-Murphy point out that the dates of beastly earthly happenings pivot around the number 666 (i.e. six hundred and sixty-six). Apparently there were nasty, but eventually abortive, manifestations around AD 666 and AD 1332 (2x666). But the big one, according to "all genuine occult tradition" (*sic*), was due in AD 1998 (3x666) with the physical birth of the Antichrist. Apparently, 'he' has to become an adult before the effects can be fully realised. Do we recognise him in our current world?

There are many doomsday predictions involving calendrical manipulations of 666 and other biblical numbers. Some are patently ridiculous and fodder for the gullible. Others are more interesting but may have little more substance. Many of the predicted dates for apocalyptic events have come and gone, apparently without any particularly striking concurrences – at least nothing over and above the normally stormy and largely unpredictable course of human history.

My Little 666 Revelation

This is a convenient point at which to introduce my own discovery about the nature of 666 (Chapter 1) – and an interpretation which may be slightly less bizarre than some. If the number was meant to contain a message for later ages and civilisations then the originator had to ensure that it was sufficiently self-contained. Perhaps no definite assumptions could be made then about the number base that might be used in the future. The number could point to its own number base – perhaps multiples of 6. It cannot be 6 because a base 6 system requires only five numerals apart from 0 (Chapter 2). It could be 12, but perhaps more obviously 18, as this is the sum of 6 + 6 + 6. The reference to 666 occurs in verse 18 of chapter 13 of Revelation – probably a coincidence.

The octodecimal number 666 (i.e. 666_{6+6+6}) is the equivalent of the decimal number 2058.

$$(6 \times 18^2) + (6 \times 18) + 6 = 2058$$

i.e.: 666 base 18 = 2058 base 10

There is something remarkable about the decimal number 2058, and therefore its equivalent octodecimal number 666. They factorise exactly into the following series of small prime numbers:

$$2 \times 3 \times 7 \times 7 \times 7$$

This could be a code requiring symbolic interpretation. The most striking and relevant component is the triple heptad, [7 x

7 x 7]. This might represent that inevitable or immutable path defined in one system as the seven conditions of consciousness, the seven conditions of life and the seven conditions of form. It may relate to the mysterious triple heptad of seals, trumpets and bowls in Revelation. The [2 x 3] component might symbolise the two opposing trinities and the forces they represent – perhaps the area in which humankind can exercise choice in the way it travels its path. The presence of the two 'trinities' together with the triple heptad within the code 666 (base 18) may be a reminder that evil and good, or chaos and harmony, are the competing driving forces in our *cosmic evolution*. Perhaps both are necessary – essentially the Manichaean principle, or in ancient Chinese philosophy, the *yin* and *yang*.

Some wag will no doubt make a more specific interpretation and decide that this provides yet another simplistic date for doomsday, or the appearance of the Antichrist – 2,058 AD? How easy it is to lose control of one's imagination! But who knows?

This may be nothing more than a strange numerological coincidence, but few other numbers derived from the digits 666 can produce such an interesting and pertinent array of small prime numbers. The argument cannot be thrown out on the basis that the ancients knew little about number bases. They may not have thought about them in the same way as modern mathematicians but they did use different bases and, ironically, some may have been particularly adept at such manipulations through the use of abaci and counting boards. Neither was there a universal premium on the use of the base 10 system. Another objection might be that the translation and interpolation from the Greek biblical manuscripts gives the number six hundred and sixty-six, which is a decimal number. But it has been broken down as 600 + 60 + 6 and perhaps this was the easiest way to present the conundrum in a clandestine but essentially decipherable form.

There is a possibility that such messages were intentionally hidden in Revelation. Some may have been transported in from more ancient sources – 666 may be one such code. However, this does not necessarily give it divine or supernatural provenance, or the need for a government health warning. But, whatever its origin, it might still contain a significant covert message.

Chapter 7
Mindset

Throughout recorded history, prophets and mystics have attempted to foretell cataclysmic and apocalyptic events. I shall use the term 'seer', in order also to include those who may not claim *divine* or *spiritual* input. The predictions of seers have covered a range of events, large and small, natural and supernatural. There are sometimes references to 'the end of the world' – but which world, whose world? Often, such predictions have focused on the smaller worlds of particular groups, rather than the whole of humanity. Over the last millennium there have been some thirty wars recorded with a million or more deaths, several with tens of millions of deaths. Half of these *recorded* wars were in the last 200 years. There are also the many *less-reported* genocides that have occurred in recent times, and are still occurring, involving tens- or hundreds-of-thousands of deaths. In addition to these *apocalyptic* events, there are the plagues and famines that have slaughtered millions throughout history. But, there seems to have been a degree of selectivity in the clairvoyant predictions of many seers – perhaps some target groups were considered more important than others. Or, perhaps the mystical *akashic record* is not so 'all-seeing' after all.

Many seers have claimed extrasensory and clairvoyant powers. Some were frauds, tempting susceptible people into their flocks with prophecies of doomsday, and promises of salvation and an afterlife. Even some of these believed that they had special powers of prediction. When nothing cataclysmic occurred on the predicted date, they sometimes blamed an error in calculation and produced a revised date. Some such seers have belonged to well-known cults and religious organisations, many of which are still flourishing today.

What exactly is a premonition, or clairvoyance? It's a difficult area, with several possible interpretations. Whilst organic brain disease or mental aberration might be a factor in a few claiming such powers, it would be naïve and ludicrous to label all prophets and psychics as deluded or insane. There may, in some, be extrasensory communications with divine or mystical spirits – the possibility cannot be discounted. There are also those whom I shall term 'sensitives' – individuals with extraordinary perceptual and pattern-recognition abilities. As with those possessing exquisite artistic and musical talents, of which most of us can only dream, there are also those who are much better at *reading* people and situations. Some might call this a 'sixth sense', but it is really an ability to use perceptual and cognitive processes (conscious and unconscious) to glean more information via the usual senses. Thus, some 'sensitives' may be better at playing poker, or predicting market trends. Some have found special roles in the 'Intelligence Services' – for instance, using an exceptional ability to pick out suspicious individuals in crowds. Some famous *psychics* were probably 'sensitives'. Not unreasonably, they may themselves have assumed that they had *mystical* powers.

There are also induced mental states during which one might have a *revelation* – states such as trance and transcendental meditation, and those following the use of certain psychoactive chemicals. Many people find that 'sleeping on a problem' often leads to a solution. Despite great advances in neuroscience, many aspects of the workings of the human brain are still poorly understood, especially in the realms of the subconscious, and the *collective unconscious*, mind.

The Universe may go on for ever and ever – who knows? However, we do not need access to the *akashic record* to predict that, one-day, our physical Earth probably *will* be destroyed by a cosmic or solar disaster, or by a huge comet or other object crossing the Earth's path. Modern astronomers and cosmologists try to keep a lookout for these threats. If we are lucky, such an event may not happen for thousands of years. Ancient astronomers may have noted past close encounters, and even made estimates of possible future returns. The ruling elite in those cultures may have incorporated religious and astrological considerations into their predictions. Unfortunately, important details may since have been lost, destroyed or misinterpreted. This has not deterred some modern enthusiasts from making questionable apocalyptic predictions based on the remaining available information, or misinformation. Modern interpreters of ancient clues and records may try to be *scientifically* objective, but this is difficult without full knowledge of the people involved and their mindsets and beliefs.

Procrustes Rides Out

There may be covert predictions and messages hidden away in the writings of seers, such as Nostradamus, and in ancient texts, such as the Pentateuch in the Old Testament. The Revelation of John provides puzzling material which may be interpreted in different ways, such as doomsday prophecies involving the millennium. Some scholars, and others, have searched such material for predictions of events that have already occurred – a sort of validation. They look for statements and correlations that appear to support the sought conclusion – a form of backward chaining. There may sometimes be a temptation, or a subconscious tendency, to be selective with antecedent statements, and to trim and re-interpret them, until they support the argument.

Nostradamus (Michel de Nostredame, 1503 – 1566 AD), a French Catholic with Jewish ancestry, was an apothecary, astrologer and seer. He is particularly famous for 'The Prophecies', a work consisting of 942 quatrains (4-line verses) which allegedly contain predictions of wars, plagues and many other events. It borrows from other authors and from the Bible. The quatrains are difficult to interpret because the statements are vague, ambiguous or even unintelligible, were written (originally) in more than one language (including a local dialect) and have probably subsequently been inaccurately translated. Dates of predicted events are rarely precisely specified, but some enthusiasts think astrological references may give clues. Not surprisingly, many previous and current fans of Nostradamus have adopted the Procrustean approach of chopping and stretching until the data fits the required result. One recent interpretation, reported on the Internet, claims that the coronavirus pandemic of 2020 was predicted. Tellingly, prospective predictions based on interpretations of the 'The Prophecies' have been unimpressive.

For centuries, Jewish scholars have searched for hidden messages encoded in the ancient Hebrew text of the Pentateuch (Torah) – the so-called Bible Code. Some feel that it should not be used as a vehicle for the prediction of future events, but this has not deterred others. A key method involves lining up a block of characters (several hundred) in horizontal and vertical rows, and then applying the *Equidistant Letter Sequence* (ELS) technique. Sequences of characters equally spaced in rows, columns and diagonals are examined (reading forwards or backwards, up or down) for relevant statements, names, dates and so on. Different blocks of text are searched until *meaningful* associations are found. Modern computing and search techniques can perform thousands of such tests in a few minutes. Michael Drosnin's books on *The Bible Code* have popularised this method as a means of prediction. He and his associates have produced some amazing retrospective predictions on all sorts of situations. Unfortunately, or perhaps fortunately, attempts at *prospective* prediction have generally, so far, been a little disappointing.

Seer Beware

There are dangers in making prospective predictions, especially of the deaths of particular people, or of wars against specific groups or cultures. This may encourage some to help fulfil the prophecy. Deluded or mentally-ill individuals, or people with a grudge, may feel impelled to carry out the predicted attack. Or, the target may feel threatened and take countermeasures.

Some religious organisations proscribed prophecy. Seers were then in danger of accusations of heresy or witchcraft. This is thought to be a reason for the covert nature of the prophecies of Nostradamus.

Chapter 8
Apocalypse When?

There have been scores of *doomsday* prophecies for dates in the last millennium (i.e. between 1000 and 2000 AD). Many of the seers had religious connections. Others included esoteric practitioners, such as occultists and astrologers. The prophecies included wide-scale death and destruction, and various supernatural occurrences, such as the second coming of Christ, or the Antichrist. *Prospective* prophecies of major apocalypses have generally failed to materialise. There may be odd concurrences with lesser events, but given the frequency of the ups-and-downs of human affairs and natural events, these could have occurred by chance.

There is an obsession with the arithmetic *millennium*. The Jewish calendar starts with Creation in 3,760 BCE. Apparently, six millennia later, in the Jewish year AM 6000 (= 2239-2240 CE), the Messianic age begins. The Messiah will then reign for a thousand years, bringing peace and love to the Earth. The Christian churches vary in their interpretation of the *Millennium*. The Catholic Church generally rejects millennialism. For others, the Second Coming of Christ occurs either before the start of the *Millennium*, or after it, coinciding with the *Day of Judgement*. When considering the Second Coming of Christ, the time period is sometimes calculated from the date of the Resurrection (assumed to be 33 AD).

Encouraged by Revelation, some have predicted events on dates involving millennia and/or 666 – for instance: 1000, 1332 (2x666), 1666, 1998 (3x666; page 59) and 2000 AD. There are claims (from *retrospective* interpretations) that Nostradamus predicted the Great Fire of London, which occurred in 1666 AD. This event was preceded by the Great Plague of London, which started in 1665 and may have killed 100,000 people. The close concurrence of these events with a date containing '666' led some to believe, at the time, that worse was to come. Although the Great Fire probably started accidentally in a bakery, some took the opportunity to accuse foreigners of starting it on purpose. The Black Death (1346-1353 AD), the disastrous pandemic which may have killed over 100 million people, appears to have been largely overlooked by earlier seers. But, it did start soon after the spooky 1332 date!

There was a plethora of failed apocalyptic predictions concerning the years around 2000 AD and 2012 AD (see page 34). Dubious pseudoscientific justifications also played a role in the spread of misinformation. At least, it was good for book sales. Perhaps we should take more notice of *bona fide* academic organisations that attempt to predict our future based on reasonably sound facts and good scholarship. Such predictions may also be uncertain, but at least they should be relatively free from *hocus pocus*. The Centre for Study of Existential Risk, at Cambridge University, is one such organisation studying the factors that might lead to future devastating catastrophes affecting human life and civilisation. Of particular interest are the causes that we can do something about – anthropogenic causes, those due to human activities. One does not need to be a 'sensitive' to work out the main concerns. They include: the development and misuse of more advanced AI systems, aberrant biotechnology, environmental disasters and global warming, overpopulation, sustainable food supplies, and appropriate governance.

The Information Battle

There is an inescapable truth about the main *spirit* behind modern human evolution. The clues come from sources as diverse as the Revelation of St. John, occultism and modern science. It may not provide the psychological refuge of religious and esoteric movements – and yet, it may underly their very existence and purpose. It is *information* and the battle for human minds. *Apocalypses* take many forms. They can be nodes of evolution, points of divergence. The tragic millennial cults waiting for divine intervention to project them, the chosen ones, to a place of safety and sweetness, for ever and ever, may actually be taking a shortcut to evolutionary dead-end. But what waits for the rest? The 21st Century will bring information (and misinformation) battles on scales never before known. In their wake may come profound divergencies in human evolution. The *Horsemen of the Apocalypse* ride on, and on.

Last Chance Saloon?

Some believe that the human brain is the most complex thing in our universe (how can they know?). But, the rapid evolutionary development of our cerebral cortex may also be associated with some potentially problematic characteristics, perhaps requiring ever-increasing control. The development of language, the 'I-am', and all that, seems to have facilitated some of the more unpleasant features of Darwinian evolution. The memes are at war! Are humans a failed experiment? Will the *gods* decide to end this *cosmic cycle* and try again? Or, will internet technology and artificial intelligence eventually bring individual humans (the *cells*) and their societies (the *organs*) together under stricter control within a new *Global Being*?

Divine Beings, if they exist, may not wish to help us clear up the mess of our own making. Overpopulation, greed, waste, pollution, war, ever-more dangerous technologies, misinformation, frictions between rival religious and political factions, and the lust for wealth and power all contribute to the major problems on our planet. You don't need a degree, or divine inspiration, to predict the outcome if we do nothing to curb these trends. Unfortunately, humans have a habit of not seeing, or not wanting to see, the elephants in the room. Aside from the ever-present, but hopefully remote, threat of a major cosmological or geological disaster, there may still be an opportunity to ensure a safer life for most people for many generations to come. But, there may be only a few years left to sort out the problems and to halt the, otherwise, almost inevitable course towards widespread and major anthropogenic apocalyptic events before the end of this century.

Human evolution is on an unpalatable and dangerous course. The aberrant behaviours of individuals, and groups, may need more effective control. But cultures differ on what is, or is not, acceptable behaviour. The *righteous*, on all sides, will need to get together soon, and show more give-and-take. Or, will humans just continue on as usual?

It's up to us!

Hocus pocus, or not, perhaps 666_{18} contains a more pertinent message than 666_{10}.

Bibliography

Aveni, A.F., *Empires of Time: Calendars, Clocks and Cultures*; I.B. Tauris & Co. Ltd., London, 1990.

Blackmore, S., *Conversations on Consciousness*; Oxford University Press, Oxford, 2005.

Blavatsky, H.P., *Isis Unveiled: Volume II – Theology*; Theosophical Publishing House, Illinois, 1972 (originally published in 1877).

Blavatsky, H.P., *The Secret Doctrine: The Synthesis of Science, Religion and Philosophy*; Volumes 1 & 2; Forgotten Books, London, 2008 (originally published in 1888).

Burke, T.P., *The Major Religions*; Blackwell Publishing Ltd., Oxford, 1996.

Caird, G.B., *The Revelation of St. John the Divine*; A. & C. Black, London, 1966.

Capra, F., *The Tao of Physics*; Flamingo, London, 1992.

Cawthorne, N., *Cults*; Quercus Editions Ltd., London, 2019.

Conway, D., *Secret Wisdom*: Jonathan Cape, London, 1987.

Davies, P., *About Time*; Penguin Books Ltd., London, 1995.

Dawkins, R., *The God Delusion*; Transworld Publishers, London, 2006.

Distin, K., *The Selfish Meme: A Critical Reassessment*; Cambridge University Press, Cambridge, 2005.

Drosnin, M., *The Bible Code*; Weidenfeld & Nicholson, UK, 1997.

Drosnin, M., *The Bible Code II: The Countdown*; Weidenfeld & Nicholson, UK, 2002.

Drosnin, M., *The Bible Code III: The Quest*; Weidenfeld & Nicholson, UK, 2006.

Farrer, A., *The Revelation of St. John the Divine*; Clarendon Press, Oxford, 1964.

Franz, von, M-L., *Time: Rhythm & Repose*; Thames & Hudson Ltd., London, 1979.

Gilbert, A. & Cotterell, M., *The Mayan Prophecies: Unlocking the Secrets of a Lost Civilization*; Element Books Ltd., Shaftesbury, UK, 1995.

Hawking, S., *A Brief History of Time*; Transworld Publishers, London, 2016.

Jaroszkiewicz, G., *Images of Time*; Oxford University Press, Oxford, 2016.

Jung, C.G., *Man and his Symbols*; Aldus Books Ltd., London, 1964.

King, J., *The Celtic Druids' Year*; Blandford, London, 1994.

Lawrence, D.H., *Apocalypse*; Penguin Books Ltd., London, 1995.

Lemesurier, P., *The Great Pyramid Decoded*; Compton Russell Ltd., Great Britain, 1977.

Mann, A.T., *Millennium Prophecies: Predictions for the Year 2000*; Element Books Ltd., Shaftesbury, UK, 1992.

McLeish, J., *Number*; Bloomsbury Publishing Ltd., London, 1991.

Ravenscroft, T. & Wallace-Murphy, T., *The Mark of the Beast*; Sphere Books Ltd., 1990.

Rowan-Robinson, M., *Ripples in the Cosmos*; W.H. Freeman & Co. Ltd., Oxford, 1993.

Scholem, G.G., *Major Trends in Jewish Mysticism* (3rd Edition); Thames & Hudson Ltd., London, 1955.

Steiner, R., *Occult Science – An Outline*; Anthroposophic Press, New York, 1950.

Steiner, R., *The Apocalypse of St. John*; Anthroposophical Publishing Company, London, 1958.

Sweet, J., *Revelation*; SCM Press, London, 1979.

Swete, H.B., *Apocalypse of St. John*; MacMillan & Co. Ltd., London, 1911.

Thompson, J.E., *Maya Chronology: The Correlation Question*; Contributions to American Archaeology, No.14, 1935.

Wells, D., *The Penguin Dictionary of Curious and Interesting Numbers*; Penguin Books Ltd., England, 1986.

Index

abacus 6, 61
AD (notation) 31
Adam Kadmon 28
Ages of civilisation 52, 53
Agrippa 57
akashic record 17, 50, 51, 64
Al-Khwarizmi 7
anthroposophy 44, 50-53
Antichrist 1, 48, 55-61, 69
apocalypse 1, 36, 63, 65,70, 71
Apocalypse of St John 3, 35-53
Arab scholars 7
archetypes 25
Aristotle 18
astral body 27, 44, 45, 51
astrology 16, 23, 65, 66, 69
astronomy 9, 16, 31, 32, 65
Atlantis 9, 17, 52, 53

atomic clock 30

Babylonian 5, 7, 15, 18, 26, 52, 58
backward chaining 66
baktun 33
bases, number 6, 13
BC (notation) 31
BCE (notation) 31
Beast, first 2, 43, 54, 55, 59
Beast, second 54, 55, 59
Bede, Venerable 31
Behemoth 54
Bible 2, 21, 35, 38, 66
Bible Code 67
binary code 14
binary system 13, 14
Black Death 70
black horse 44-49

Blavatsky, Helena 50
Bowls 39-46, 53
Buddhism 26

caesium-133 clock 30
calendars 6, 30-34
Caligula 55
Canon, the 37
Capra, Fritjof 28
CE (notation) 31
Celtic 11, 18
chakras 27
Chaldean 26, 52
Chinese 7, 13, 14, 20, 21
Christ, Jesus 22, 31, 36-45, 48, 69, 70
Christian(s) 7, 18, 32, 36, 37, 40, 44, 45, 48, 50, 57
Christ Principle, the 45
clairvoyance 17, 40, 50, 51, 64
collective unconscious, the 25, 40, 65
cosmic evolution 49, 61, 72
cosmology 28, 65

Darwin 50, 72
decimal system 6, 10, 13
denary 13
Divine, the 27, 28, 72
Divine Proportion 11, 12
dodecahedron 20
Domitian 37
doomsday prophecies 66, 69, 70
Druids 18
duodecimal system 13, 14
dyadic 13

ego 27, 44, 45

Egyptian 5-13, 18, 32, 52, 58
ELS method 67
Empedocles 26
epochs 46, 51-53
esoteric 17, 18, 27, 51
evolution 41, 50, 53, 59, 71, 72
exegesis 39, 41
Exiguus, Dionysius 31
exoteric 45
extrasensory 64

Fibonacci 7, 12
Francesca, Piero della 11

gematria 22
genocides 63
Gideon Bible 2, 56
Global Being 72
Globes 26, 51, 52
God 14, 20, 21, 27, 39, 41, 46, 51
golden section 11, 12, 13
great cycle 33, 34
Great Fire of London 70
Great Plague of London 70
Greek(s) 7-11, 22, 37, 57
Gregorian Calendar 31, 33

Hebrew 8, 22, 52, 57, 59, 67
Hinduism 7, 26
Horsemen, the 42, 46-50, 71
hexadecimal system 13, 14
hexagesimal system 13, 15

'I', the (or 'I am') 44, 45, 49, 51,72
Indian 5, 7, 9, 13, 18, 52
information 14, 48, 50, 71, 72
irrational numbers 10, 25
isopsephia 22

Jesus – see Christ
Jews, Jewish 7, 21, 38, 44, 57, 69
John, the Apostle 36
John, the Elder 36
John of Patmos 37, 39, 40, 54
Julian Calendar 31
Jung, Carl 25, 40

Kabbalah 18, 22, 27

Lamb, the 36, 41-44
Later Heaven 21
Lawrence, D.H. 36
Leibnitz 11, 14
Lemurians 17
letter-numbers 7, 8
Leonardo da Pisa – see Fibonacci
Leviathan 54
Liber Abaci 7, 12
long count 33
Lo Shu 21

machine code 14
magic square 20, 21, 58
Manichaean 61
Maya, Mayan 9, 15, 32-34
Mesoamerica 32, 34
millennium 41, 69, 70
Moses 21

Neo-Platonists 18
Nero 22, 37, 55, 57
New-Age 23, 51
New Testament 21, 35, 36, 41
Newton, Isaac 30
Nostradamus 66-68, 70
notarikon 22
number

666: ix, 1-3, 20, 22, 55-62, 70, 73
777: 24, 26, 40, 43, 58, 60
bases 13-15, 60
golden section 11-13
irrational 10, 25
perfect 10
prime 10, 60
rational 10, 25
real 10
square 19
triangular 19, 20, 58
numerology 4, 16, 22-24

occult, occultism 2, 3, 16, 17, 26, 27, 41-45, 69, 71
octodecimal system 60
Old Testament 21, 35-40, 48, 54, 57
Olmec 33

pale horse 46-49
Palenque 9, 32
pentagram 12, 13
Pentateuch 21, 66, 67
phi 11-13
pi 11
Planetary stage 26, 51, 52
Plato 17, 18
Plotinus 18
prime numbers 10, 60
Procrustes 24, 66
Prophecies, The (of Nostradamus) 66-68
prophets, prophecy 31, 34, 38, 39, 42, 63, 64, 68
pseudoscience 70
psychics 65

Pythagoras, Pythagorean 8, 10-14, 17-22, 25

quantum physics 28

rational number 10, 25
real number 10, 25
red horse 46-49
relativity 28
Revelation 2, 3, 23, 35-55, 60, 66, 71
righteous, the 48, 73
Roman State 37, 55
Rounds 26, 51, 52

Satan 39, 41, 54, 55
Seals 39-46, 53
seer 63-69
sensitives 64, 65
singularity 29
solar year 30
Solomon 57
Spirit 44-46, 49, 53, 54, 63, 64, 71
square numbers 19
Steiner, Rudolf 44, 46, 49-53, 59

Sumer 5
Sun God 57

Talmud 21
tetraktys 19
theosophy 50
time 29-34
Tree of Life 27
triangular numbers 19, 20, 58
Trinity
    Holy 27, 54, 61
    Satanic 27, 54, 61
triple heptads 26, 40, 43, 58, 60, 61
Trumpets 39-46, 53

vigesimal system 13, 15, 32, 33
Vinci, Leonardo da 11

wars 42, 63
white horse 46-50
woes 43
Word, the 48, 50

yin & yang 61